Reekin' Ramp Recipes

Reekin' Ramp Recipes

Barbara Beury McCallum

Charleston, WV

Quarrier Press
Charleston, WV

©2010, Barbara Beury McCallum

All rights reserved. No part of this book may be reproduced in any form or means, electronic or mechanical, including photocopying, recording, or by any information storage and retrieval system, without permission in writing from the publisher.

Book and cover design: Mark S. Phillips

Library of Congress Control Number: 2010925355
ISBN 13: 978-1-891852-68-8
ISBN 10: 1-891852-68-x

10 9 8 7 6 5 4 3 2

Printed in the United States of America

Distributed by:

West Virginia Book Co.
1125 Central Avenue
Charleston, WV 25302

www.wvbookco.com

Dedication:

The following devotees of the West Virginia ramp deserve special recognition for their support of this cookbook in its first edition:

> The late Jim Comstock—writer, humorist, and West Virginian historian, Mr. Comstock created and edited the *West Virginia Hillbilly*.

> The late Dr. Earl L. Core—Dr. Core was professor of Botany at West Virginia University, and author of *Flora of West Virginia* and *Spring Wildflowers of West Virginia*.

Table of Contents

Introduction 9
Ramps: For Breath You Can Slice With a Knife
　Alyce Faye Bragg 17
Fried Ramps and Potatoes 21
Pickled Ramps 21
Beef Choufleur Et Ramps 22
Mountaineer Hash 23
Ramp Corn Bread 24
Fried Ramps I 25
Fried Ramps II 25
Ramps with Bacon and Eggs 26
Ramp Soup 27
Poor Man's Ramp Stew 28
Spanish Rampin' Meatloaf 29
Open Face Sandwich 30
Ramps as a Vegetable 30
Ramp Salad 31
Ramp Canapés 31
Ramp Hors D'oeuvre 32
Ramp Grits Soufflé 33
Braised Chicken with Ramps 35
Ramp Pancakes—Chinese Style 37
Spaghetti with Ramp Sauce 39
Potato and Ramp Omelet 40
Ramp Champs (Mashed Potatoes with Ramps) 42
Ramp Soup with Eggs 44
Gourmet Ramp Soup 45

Asparagus, Morels, and Ramp Salad 47
Ramp Hushpuppies 48
Roasted Chicken, Ramps, and Potatoes 49
White Cheese Pizza with Ramps 51
Grilled Tuna with Ramps, Pinto Beans and Tomato
    Vinaigrette 53
Ramp Pesto 55
Spaghetti Sauce with Ramps 56
Ramp Casserole 57
Ramp and Buttermilk Biscuits 58
Scalloped Potatoes with Ramps 59
Macaroni Salad with Ramps 60
Three-Way Appetizer Spread 61
Crockpot Smothered Steak with Ramps 62
Quick Ramp Vichyssoise 63
Wilted Lettuce and Ramp Salad 64
Sour Cream Potato Salad with Ramps 65
Cream of Potato/Ramp Soup 66
Pork Ribs with Ramps and Peppers 67
Swiss Ramp Quiche 68
Easy Ramp Flatbreads 69
Tomato, Spinach and Ramp Penne 70
Ramp Aioli 71

Introduction

"Eat leeks in Lide (March) and ramsins in May, and all the year after physicians may play."

Ramps. People familiar with the smelly, leafy and bulbous ramp usually have strong feelings about them, either positive or negative, because of their odor. One hillbilly solution to avoiding the intense smell of ramps on other people's breath: "eat 'em your self." Since the plant's consumption in late winter and early spring is widely thought to improve your health, the question arises: Are the health benefits and/or its taste sufficient to justify living with the odor?

The late great West Virginia writer Jim Comstock had this to say about the ramp and its odor: "Don't let the horror stories about ramp odor scare you off....... a ramp is just an onion that hasn't been civilized or had the fear of the Lord driven into it; it's Nature's best evidence that He who made the lamb also made the tiger."

Comstock, the editor of the *West Virginia Hillbilly*, created a controversy one year by mixing ramp juice into the ink for a festival edition of Richwood's other paper, the *News-Leader*. Mail clerks complained, as did many others. The result was the postmaster sending Comstock a terse letter, stating it was beyond the call of duty for the postmaster and his staff to have to accept and handle offensive-smelling mail.

And if you think the Richwood postal service was

especially sensitive, or that Mountaineers simply like to play up the lowly ramp's smell, read what William Shakespeare said of the plant: "By this leek, I will most horribly revenge. I eat and eat, I swear." –*King Henry V,* Act V, scene 1, line 49

So we know the plant made an impact sufficient to warrant mention by England's great bard. Actually, the plant appears again and again throughout history, from the Brothers Grimm in their German fairy tale *Rapunzel,* to French explorers in America's Great Lakes region.

In *Rapunzel,* the pregnant mother in the fairy tale craves an herb called rampion so badly that she thinks she'll die without it. Her obedient husband scales the wall surrounding the witch's garden and steals some leaves. The botanical name for rampion is the Latin *campanula rapunculus*— which translates to *ramponzolo* or *raponzo* in medieval Italian—and *raiponce* in French. Rapunzel is the German name for the plant.

When the prince is caught by the witch, he agrees to trade away his yet unborn child to the witch in return for a steady supply of rapunzel for his wife. The witch names the infant Rapunzel after the herb.

The medieval appetite for rapunzel was not usually for its leaves, but the plant's thick, fleshy roots. Before the potato came to Europe, the foot long roots of *campanula rapunculus* were cooked as a starchy food. In the spring, when rapunzel's leaves were tender and fresh, they were also used in salads. But once potato production became common in Europe, rapunzel largely retreated from the kitchen.

Here on our soil, the North American variety of ramp, *allium tricoccum*, typically grows from Canada and Minnesota in the north; and as far south as the mountains of North Carolina and Tennessee. In West Virginia, extensive beds of ramps are found in the rich mountain woodlands, particularly in the Monongahela National Forest, which runs along the state's eastern boundary and is designated in our state as the "heart of Ramp Country." Ramps grow best in areas of heavy snow and cooler temperatures.

The ramp's broad, flat leaves resemble the lily-of-the-valley; its thin stem and pearly white bulb are reminiscent of the wild onion. Ramp leaves appear in the early spring, but by June and July, when its delicate white flowers appear, its leaves have long withered and disappeared.

In pioneer days, Appalachian mountain people were drawn to the plant to supplement their monotonous winter food supply, which consisted largely of cornpone, salt pork, molasses, and dried vegetables, supplemented by occasional wild game. In mid-March, after a long winter and still no fresh green vegetables in sight, the appearance of the ramps' pale green leaves in the still frozen ground was much heralded.

The name of the plant has several similar, but slightly varied, origins. One foreign relative, the French wild leek or *rampion*, is highly prized in gourmet cooking. Another English relative, the *ramson*, is commonly called the European bear leek or *allium ursinum*. This broad-leaved species of garlic is similar to our American plant, and much cultivated and eaten in salads.

Further back, the word ramson came from the Anglo-Saxon *hramsa*, related to *rams* in German, Danish, Swedish and Norwegian. Interestingly, the zodiac sign of Aries, Arabic for ram, is the male sheep, known to be stout, rambunctious, and a bit odiferous. The zodiac dates for Aries, March 21 – April 21, coincide with the first appearance of those precious ramp leaves, eaten by sturdy mountain goats and human foragers alike. Thus it was concluded that eating ramps in the early spring is "good for what ails you," and they are still consumed as a spring tonic.

The ramp is occasionally and confusingly known as a "wild onion," Indian turnip," or "leek." Though a relative of the onion, garlic, and chive, the ramp has a sharp difference in taste, growth pattern, and smell. Another nickname for the plant's white bulb is "Devils turnip."

The ramp also merits mention in the first written record of the origin of Chicago, Illinois, in the journal of Henri Joutel, the historian of La Salle's expedition of 1684-87. During an exploration in early spring, Joutel describes how the party subsisted largely on "wild garlic," which was later proven to be the wild leek or ramp. The plants were so common that they gave the place the Indian name *shikako* or *checagou*, which means "the place of the wild garlic."

Many people continue to be offended by the rather strong,

lingering odor associated with ramp eaters. But after a two or three day waiting period, the ramp eater is usually sufficiently odorless enough to re-enter society.

Ramps are excellent raw, although they are usually parboiled and seasoned or fried with bacon grease. In Appalachia, ramp "feeds" in early spring are not only a chance to have a highly nutritious meal, but eating this unusual, indigenous food also lets us identify with our ancestors.

Every spring, ramp dinners are held all over the state. The big daddy dinner in West Virginia occurs during the town of Richwood's ***Feast of the Ramson.*** For information on the Richwood dinner, call 304-846-6790.

The town of Elkins hosts the ***International Ramp Festival***, usually on the first weekend in April. For information on the Elkins festival, call 304-636-2780. Two other large festivals include the Pickens Ramp Dinner (call 304-924-5415); and the Helvetia Ramp Dinner (call 304 924-6435.)

Plenty of other towns around the state also host ramp festivals and dinners, so check your local newspaper. Each festival has its own unique atmosphere. While music and local entertainment is often provided, state politicians and national celebrities can sometimes be spotted at the dinners.

Other colloquial names for a ramp dinner are a ramp whiff, a ramp romp, or just a plain old stink supper, where presumably you will eat a "messaramps."

One wives' tale says you can tell if you are near a ramp dinner if you see skunks fleeing down the road; they hate the smell of ramps. Another historic way to spot a "stink supper" is to look up in the sky: if you see a horde of buzzards circling in early spring, chances are good a ramp feed is going on directly below.

Woman's Day ran an article on ramps in May 1956, part of which is quoted here: "Perhaps one citizen in 30,000 has tasted ramps, and there may be one in 60,000 who likes them. They are described as a cross between onions and garlic, except that onions and garlic are a whisper and ramps are a Comanche war whoop. . . the innocent looking little ramp is the most violent of vegetables."

It's just too easy to pick on the ramp because of its odor: heck, a number of businesses (think Trident and Listerine) have been built upon the stigma of having even a weak onion for lunch. And what mortal hasn't heard of warding off vampires with garlic? An English dictionary from 1904 read as follows, "On these hills is found a mountain leek, or *ramsh* as it is here named (in Perthshire), whereupon the goats feed, and sometimes their milk smells of it." A more complete description has described the ramp's essence as a combination of goat sweat, sour milk and battery acid. Wow.

Franklin Roosevelt, Jr., apparently didn't have a stomach for goat sweat, et al. The 1960 presidential candidate, Hubert Humphrey, and Kennedy's front man, Roosevelt, both made the trek to Richwood's Feast of the Ramson. While Humphrey entered the cafeteria and ate a huge plate of ramps, Roosevelt quickly left the cafeteria after entering, eating nothing. But the affection for or against ramps must not have carried much weight with the voters. Kennedy went on to win the West Virginia primary, a huge step on his road to the White House.

But here's the big "but." As with many things, the overlooked or the underdog can still evolve into the greatest hit. Even though the ramp has been popular among gourmands in Europe and mountain folk everywhere for centuries, it's been pretty much ignored by cooks in general. No more.

Now the lowly ramp has gone prime time. It's been featured in recipes on NPR's *The Splendid Table*; television's *Iron Chef*, many gourmet magazines, and served in some of the nation's top restaurants.

Today, the humble green can be found in such delicacies as *Tuna Steaks Grilled with Ramps*, *White Cheese Pizza with Ramps*, and *Ramp Pesto*, among others.

And with more people becoming aware of ramps, new recipes and uses have emerged. You can now even purchase commercially produced ramp wine. And as odd as it sounds, and as strong as it smells, it goes down pretty darn good.

So if you haven't had the opportunity or the nerve to try ramps, don't put it off any longer. Try them in one of these fancy dishes if you must turn your nose up at traditional ramp fare. But the lowdown? Ramps *are* totally worth the hype. And with a colorful history stretching from Germany's Middle Ages to pioneer America, what are you waiting for?

Ramps: For Breath You Can Slice with a Knife
by Alyce Faye Bragg

Some people feel that springtime is not complete without a good mess of ramps. Ramps are a true mountain food, relished by many and scorned by some. I belong to the former group.

The dictionary tells us that they are a wild, onion-like plant found in eastern North America with a characteristically strong odor; eaten by mountain folk during some of their spring festivals in the latter part of April. As the Queen of Sheba said to Solomon, "The half was not told me." Ramps cannot be adequately described; they must be experienced.

They are an innocent appearing little plant, with flat, broad leaves and a tender, white root. Ramp addicts have been known to dig under the dead leaves and unearth these delicacies before the leaf bud emerges from the ground. We had some of those this spring, too.

As for eating them at festivals, I suppose one could call ramp eating a "festival" at any time. Husband and I have enjoyed them as a cozy twosome: the *piece de resistance* of a romantic, candlelit table. (This was in a camper where the only source of light was a candle stuck in a soda pop bottle.) And it is a festive occasion when we get together as a family on our camping and fishing trips and cook ramps for everyone over an open campfire. As you drive along the road paralleling

Williams River, the aroma from the campfires mingle together into one great odorous homage to the lowly ramp.

There is another peculiar feature of this wild plant—when you feast upon these seasonal victuals, you cannot smell the odor of them on anyone else. That is why we like to indulge when we are out in open country. Fortunately, everyone in our large family likes this food. When my father was living, he liked to include everyone, from bald-headed infant to Grandpa on a cane, on his frequent camping trips. He had an enormous tent and we would be packed in at night like sardines in a tin can. Mom would pin the quilts together with big safety pins (talk about togetherness) and if one fellow had to turn over, we all had to turn. The worst place to sleep was on the sides next to the wall of the tent, as the nights were often cold, and sometimes the covers didn't stretch that far. I remember one time in particular when the whole family (married kids and their children included) plus our pastor and a few assorted friends all went with Daddy on one of his forays into the wilderness.

The men dug a gunny sack of ramps, and we had a superfluous ramp feed that evening. Mom owned a gigantic steel skillet that held about a peck of ramps at a time, and it was put to good use. Unfortunately, my baby sister Susie, who was a teen-ager at the time, didn't partake. That night, there she was zipped up in a tent with a multitude of ramp eaters. She would yell out at intervals, "Don't breathe in this direction!" and "Quit laughing—it makes it worse!" I don't know how that poor young'un survived the night. To this day, she doesn't care for ramps. I reckon that would be enough to turn a person against them forever.

I wonder if this is an acquired taste, or do you fall in love with them at first bite? I have been eating them for so long that I can't remember. When you grow up with them in your Pablum, it is hard to pinpoint that first taste.

A friend from Michigan told us that they grow in his native state, but they call them wild leeks. He recalls that when he was a boy and got tired of going to school every day, all he had to do was eat a few raw ramps and he would be invited to stay home for a few days. Raw ramps are actually the culprit when it comes to breath that you can slice with a knife. Cooked ramps actually don't linger on the breath all that long. A couple of days, maybe.

I have recipes for pickled ramps and ramp soup, if anyone is interested. I haven't tried the recipes. The only thing I like to add to ramps are eggs—and bacon, of course.

After a good mess of them, my system feels rejuvenated and I think I can make it until next spring and another ramp season. Would someone pass the Sen-Sen please?

Alyce Faye Bragg
The Charleston Gazette
Friday, April 24, 1992

Recipes

Fried Ramps and Potatoes

Clean as many ramps as you want to cook. Cut into 1-inch pieces using tops and all. Peel and slice about the same amount of potatoes as ramps. Fry together in bacon fat until done. Break 2-3 eggs over ramps and potatoes and stir through. Let mixture fry a minute or two until eggs are cooked on bottom. Turn and cook several minutes more until eggs are done. Twice as good served with homemade bread and butter.

Pickled Ramps

4 quarts cleaned ramps* (with leaves cut off)
1 quart white vinegar diluted with water
1 cup sugar
2 Tablespoons salt

Boil vinegar, sugar, and salt for ten minutes. Add ramps to mixture and continue to boil for three minutes. Put in jars and seal.
*Use ramps that are too mature for eating raw or for table use.

Beef Choufleur Et Ramps

1 pound boneless round steak, cut $1/_3$-inch thick
1 small head cauliflower
2 Tablespoons butter
1 green pepper, cut in ¾-inch pieces
¼ cup soy sauce
1 cup of finely chopped ramps (bulbs and stems)
2 Tablespoons cornstarch
½ cup sugar
1 ½ cups beef broth or water
3 cups hot cooked rice

Cut meat into ½-inch squares. Separate cauliflower into flowerettes (about 4 cups). Brown meat in butter about 5 minutes. Add cauliflower, green pepper, and soy sauce. Cover pan and simmer until vegetables are barely tender (about 10 minutes).

Blend cornstarch, sugar, and beef broth. Add to meat mixture with ramps. Cook, stirring constantly, until thoroughly heated and sauce is thickened. Serve over beds of fluffy rice.

6 servings.

Mountaineer Hash

4-5 ramps
1 medium green pepper, chopped
3 Tablespoons of butter
1 pound ground beef
2 cups canned tomatoes
1 teaspoon chili powder
¼ teaspoon pepper
1 teaspoon salt
½ cup uncooked rice

    Preheat oven to 350 degrees.
    Cook together 4-5 chopped ramps with 1 medium chopped green pepper in 3 Tablespoons of butter, until ramps are yellow. Add 1 pound of ground beef and sauté until mixture falls apart. Add 2 cups of canned tomatoes, chili powder, pepper, uncooked rice, and salt. Mix and pour into greased baking dish.
    Bake at 350 degrees for 45 minutes.
    6-8 servings.

Ramp Corn Bread

1 cup cottage cheese
1 cup cream style corn
1 cup grated cheddar cheese
1 cup self-rising corn meal
2 eggs
½ cup chopped ramps: both stems and bulbs
½ cup chopped sweet peppers
¼ cup melted shortening

Preheat oven to 350 degrees.
Combine all ingredients and bake in a well-greased pan for 1 hour at 350 degrees.

Fried Ramps I

Clean ramps and boil a few minutes. Pour off water and replace with clean water. Repeat this through three waters. Cook until tender.

Drain and put into a skillet with bacon drippings. Fry and turn a few minutes until the bacon drippings are thoroughly mixed with the ramps.

Serve with corn bread and fried potatoes.

Fried Ramps II

Parboil* cleaned ramps that have been cut into 1-inch pieces in plain water. While ramps are boiling, fry bacon in a large iron frying pan to the point just before it becomes crisp. Cut bacon into small pieces.

Drain parboiled ramps and place in the hot bacon fat. Season with salt and pepper to taste and fry until done.

Serve garnished with boiled egg slices.

Some cooks break eggs over the ramps during the final seconds of cooking and stir slightly. Remove and serve when eggs are done.

*Ramps are often cooked without boiling.

Ramps with Bacon and Eggs

1 quart diced ramps, including stems
6 strips of bacon
6 large eggs

    Wash and clean ramps as you would onions; dice medium fine. Cook in salted water until tender; drain well. Meanwhile fry the bacon until crisp; drain on paper towels, and break into small bits. Pour half the bacon drippings off; add eggs, salt to taste, and soft scramble. Stir bacon bits and scrambled eggs through ramps while hot.
    Serve immediately. 6 servings.

Ramp Soup

1 pound diced ham
18 or so ramps
4-5 pieces of celery
2-3 carrots
1 large onion
1 pound potatoes
milk
salt and pepper to taste

Bring two quarts of water to a rolling boil. Add ½ teaspoon salt and 1 pound of diced ham. Boil 10-15 minutes (if scum forms, skim it off).

Cut ramps, celery, carrots, and potatoes into small pieces and add to pot. Cook until potatoes are tender.

Add milk to consistency, salt and pepper to taste and simmer for 15-20 minutes. Use flour to thicken soup if needed.

Add butter and serve hot.
4 servings.

Poor Man's Ramp Stew

2 pounds ground beef
8 ramps, bulb and stems, chopped
5-6 large potatoes, chopped
4-5 carrots, chopped
Any other odds and ends of vegetables you may have left over

Put beef in a large soup pot and cover with water. Simmer until meat loses its redness, then add the chopped ramps, diced potatoes, and carrots.

Season to taste and cook until the vegetables are tender.

6-8 servings.

Spanish Rampin' Meatloaf

2 pounds extra-lean ground round
1 package (5.6 oz.) Spanish rice mix, prepared according to directions
2 eggs or 4 egg whites
6-8 ramp bulbs and stems finely minced
¼ teaspoon pepper
1 Tablespoon prepared mustard

Preheat oven to 350 degrees.
Combine ingredients and shape into loaf and place in shallow baking pan. Bake one hour.
8 servings.

Open Face Sandwich

Take a piece of white bread and spread with butter. Cover with several ramps cut into thin slices and serve.

Ramps as a Vegetable

Ramps are delicious boiled and served with Hollandaise or cheese sauce.

Ramp Salad

Take West Virginia mountain ramps and chop fine. Cook until tender, but do not parboil. Season with salt, ham fryings, and vinegar, and garnish with sliced hard-boiled eggs. Serve warm.

Ramp Canapés

Mix together Tabasco sauce, cream cheese, and chopped ramps and spread on rounds of melba toast or toasted bread squares and serve.

Ramp Hors D'oeuvre

1 cup shredded cheddar cheese
½ cup ripe olives (chopped)
¼ cup onions (chopped)
mayonnaise

    Mix shredded cheddar cheese, ripe olives and onions. Add enough mayonnaise to form a thick paste. Spread mixture on party rye bread and cover with finely chopped ramps bulbs.
    Heat in the broiler until cheese melts and the bread is toasted.

Ramp Grits Soufflé

1 cup hominy grits
1 teaspoon salt
¾ stick (6 Tablespoons) unsalted butter
2 large eggs
¼ pound cheddar cheese, grated
½ cup trimmed and minced ramp bulbs and stems
3 Tablespoons freshly grated Parmesan
cayenne and black pepper to taste

    Preheat oven to 350 degrees.
    In a heavy saucepan bring 3 ½ cups of water to a boil. Stir in the grits in a stream with the salt. Simmer the mixture covered for 25 minutes, or until thick, stirring occasionally.
    Remove the pan from the heat, add 4 Tablespoons of the butter, cut into pieces, and stir the mixture until the butter is melted. Add the eggs one at a time, beating well as you add them, then stir in the cheddar cheese.
    In a small skillet, cook the ramps in the remaining 2 Tablespoons of butter over moderately low heat, stirring until the ramps are softened. Stir the mixture into the grits with the Parmesan, cayenne and pepper to taste, and transfer the mixture to a buttered 1 ½-quart soufflé dish.
    Put dish in a baking pan, add enough hot water

to the pan to reach halfway up the sides of the dish, and bake the soufflé in the middle of a preheated oven at 350 degrees for 1 hour, or until it is puffed and golden.

    6 servings.

— Reprint from Gourmet, *April 1983*

Braised Chicken with Ramps

3-pound chicken, cut into serving pieces
2 Tablespoons unsalted butter
2 Tablespoons vegetable oil
1 small onion, minced
½ cup dry Vermouth
2 ounces ramp bulbs, trimmed, reserving the green tops from 2 ramps for garnish
1 cup chicken stock or canned chicken broth
½ bay leaf
¼ teaspoon crumbled dried thyme
⅓ cup heavy cream

    Use a stainless steel or enameled skillet or shallow casserole large enough to hold the chicken in one layer. In skillet, heat the butter and the oil over moderately high heat until the fat is hot.

    Rinse, pat dry, and season the chicken with salt and pepper. Brown the chicken in the fat and transfer it with tongs to a plate. Pour off all but 2 Tablespoons of the fat from the skillet and, in the remaining fat, cook the onions over moderate heat, stirring until soft.

    Add the Vermouth, deglaze the skillet, scraping up the brown bits clinging to the bottom and sides, and reduce the liquid by half over moderately high heat. Add the ramps, the stock, bay leaf, thyme, and salt and pepper to taste. Arrange the chicken, skin side up in the skillet, and bring the liquid to a simmer. Cook the chicken at a bare simmer, covered, for 15 minutes, or until the breasts are just tender.

Transfer the breasts with a slotted spoon to a platter, and keep them warm, covered loosely. Cook the legs and the wings at a bare simmer, covered, for 5 minutes more, or until they are tender. Transfer them with a slotted spoon to the platter, and keep them warm, covered loosely.

Discard the bay leaf. In a food processor fitted with a steel blade, or in a blender, puree the cooking liquid, and strain the puree through a fine sieve into the skillet, pressing hard on the solids. Bring the liquid to a boil over moderately high heat, add the cream and salt and pepper to taste, and cook the sauce, stirring, for 1-2 minutes, or until thickened slightly.

Dab the chicken with the sauce and garnish the dish with the reserved ramp greens, minced.

4-6 servings.

— *Reprint from* Gourmet, *April 1983*

Ramp Pancakes—Chinese Style

For the dipping sauce:
- 2 Tablespoons soy sauce
- 1 Tablespoon rice wine or Scotch
- 1 Tablespoon rice vinegar* or white wine vinegar
- ¼ teaspoon peeled and grated ginger root
- ¼ teaspoon chili oil*

For the pancakes:
- 2 cups all purpose flour
- 1 teaspoon salt
- 2 Tablespoons Oriental sesame oil*
- 2 Tablespoons trimmed and minced ramps
- Peanut oil for frying

*Available at Oriental markets

Make the dipping sauce: In a small bowl combine the soy sauce, the wine, the vinegar, the ginger root, the ramps, and the chili oil.

Make the pancakes: In a heatproof bowl, combine the flour and the salt, stirring in 1 cup of boiling water, and forming the dough into a ball. Knead the dough on a floured surface until it is smooth and let stand, covered with an inverted bowl, for 30 minutes. Form the dough into a 12-inch log, cut it crosswise into 1-inch pieces, and cover the pieces with the inverted bowl.

Flatten 1 piece of the dough cut side down on a floured surface and roll it into a 4-inch round. Brush the round lightly with the sesame oil and sprinkle it with ½ teaspoon of the ramps. Roll up the round, flatten it slightly, and roll it into a 4" x 1" strip.

Beginning with the short end, roll up the strip and turn the roll coiled side up. Flatten the roll slightly and roll it gently into a 5 or 6-inch round, being careful not to tear it.

Make the pancakes with the remaining dough pieces, sesame oil, and ramps in the same manner. In a large heavy skillet at least 7 inches across the bottom, heat $1/3$ inch peanut oil over moderately high heat until it is very hot, but not smoking, and in it fry the pancakes, one at a time, turning them once, for 30 to 40 seconds, or until they are golden and bubbly.

Transfer them with a slotted spatula to paper towels to drain. Arrange the pancakes, quartered if desired, on a platter and put the bowl of dipping sauce in the center.

Serves 6 to 12 as an hors d'oeuvre.

— Reprint from Gourmet, *April 1983*

Spaghetti with Ramp Sauce

½ cup trimmed and minced ramps
½ teaspoon red pepper flakes
½ cup olive oil
½ pound spaghetti, cooked in boiling salted water until it is *al dente* and drained

    In a large heavy skillet, cook the ramps with the red pepper flakes in the oil over moderately low heat, stirring until the pepper flakes are softened. Then increase heat to moderate and cook until the ramps are golden.

    Add the spaghetti and salt and pepper to taste. Toss the mixture until the spaghetti is coated with the sauce, and transfer it to a serving bowl.

    4 servings.

— Reprint from Gourmet, *April 1983*

Potato and Ramp Omelet

8 large eggs
2 dashes of Tabasco
½ stick (¼ cup) unsalted butter

For the filling:
1 lb. new potatoes, scrubbed
¼ pound sliced lean bacon, chopped
¼ cup trimmed and thinly sliced ramps

Make the filling: In a steamer set over boiling water, steam the potatoes, covered partially, for 30-40 minutes, or until they are just tender. Let the potatoes cool, peel them if desired, and cut them into $1/3$-inch cubes.

In a heavy skillet, cook the bacon over moderate heat, stirring until crisp. Transfer the bacon with a slotted spoon to a bowl, and pour off all but 3 Tablespoons of the fat from the skillet. In the remaining fat, cook the ramps, stirring, until they are softened. Add the potatoes, bacon, salt and pepper to taste, and cook the mixture, stirring, for 3 minutes, or until the potatoes are lightly golden. Keep the filling warm, covered.

In a bowl, beat the eggs lightly with 3 Tablespoons cold water, the Tabasco, and salt to taste.

Heat an omelet pan or a non-stick skillet about 5½ inches across the bottom, over moderately high heat until it is hot and add 1 Tablespoon of butter, swirling the pan, until the foam subsides. Add one quarter of the egg mixture and cook it, undisturbed, for 5 seconds. Cook the omelet, stirring the top layer with the back of a fork and shaking the pan, until it is barely set.

Remove the pan from the heat, spoon one quarter of the filling across the center of the omelet, and loosen the edge of the omelet with a rubber spatula, shaking the pan. Fold the top third of the omelet over the filling. Then fold the bottom third over the middle, and, tilting the pan away from you, slide the omelet to the bottom of the pan. Invert the omelet onto an ovenproof serving plate and keep it warm in a preheated very slow oven (200 degrees.) Make 3 more omelets with the remaining egg mixture, filling, and butter in the same manner. Blot any liquid that has seeped from the omelets with a paper towel.

4 servings.

— Reprint from Gourmet, *April 1983*

Ramp Champs
(Mashed Potatoes with Ramps)

2 ½ lbs. baking potatoes
½ cup trimmed and minced ramp bulbs and stems
1 ¼ sticks (10 Tablespoons) unsalted butter, softened
1 ¼ cups milk
1 Tablespoon minced green ramp tops for garnish

    In a heavy saucepan, cover the potatoes with 2 inches cold water and bring the water to a boil. Add salt to taste and simmer the potatoes, covered partially, for 40 minutes, or until they are tender. Drain the potatoes, return them to the pan, and steam them dry, covered, shaking the pan, for 3 minutes. Let the potatoes cool until they can be handled and peel them.
    While the potatoes are boiling, in a small saucepan, cook the ramps in 2 Tablespoons of the butter over low heat, stirring, for 5 minutes, or until they are softened. Add the milk, scald the mixture over moderate heat, and keep warm.
    Rice the potatoes or force them through a food mill into a large saucepan and beat in 6 Tablespoons of the remaining butter, cut into pieces.

Add the milk mixture in a stream, beating, season the mixture with salt and pepper, and, if necessary, heat it over low heat, stirring, until it is heated through. Transfer the mixture to a heated serving dish, garnish it with the ramp tops, and top it with the remaining 2 Tablespoons butter.

8 servings.

— Reprint from Gourmet, *April 1983*

Ramp Soup with Eggs

6 slices of French or Italian bread (1-inch thick)
½ cup peanut oil
2/3 cup trimmed and thinly sliced ramps
6 cups chicken stock or canned chicken broth
6 large eggs at room temperature
6 heated deep soup bowls

    Brush the bread lightly with some of the oil. Toast the slices on a baking sheet in the middle of a preheated over (350 F.), turning them once, for 20 to 25 minutes, or until they are golden and crisp. Keep them warm.
    In a large heavy saucepan, cook the ramps in ¼ cup of the remaining oil over low heat, stirring, for 10 to 15 minutes, or until they are soft. Add the stock with salt to taste, bring it to a boil, and simmer the soup, covered for 5 minutes. Break 1 slice of the toast into each of the 6 heated deep soup bowls and break 1 of the eggs carefully into each bowl. Ladle the hot soup into the bowls and stir briefly.
    6 servings.

— Reprint from Gourmet, *April 1983*

Gourmet Ramp Soup

1 lb. ramps
½ sweet onion such as Vidalia, thinly sliced
¼ teaspoon white pepper
2 Tablespoons vegetable oil
1/3 cup dry white wine
3 ½ cups reduced sodium chicken broth
¼ cup grated Parmigiano-Reggiano
2 Tablespoons unsalted butter

Trim roots from the ramps and slip off outer skin on the bulbs if loose. Cut green tops from ramps and coarsely chop enough greens to measure 3 cups (reserve remainder for other use). Thinly slice ramp bulbs, including pink stems.

Cook ramp bulbs, onions, white pepper, and ½ teaspoon salt in oil in a large heavy saucepan over medium heat, stirring occasionally, until softened, about 10 minutes. Add wine, then boil over high heat, stirring occasionally, until evaporated completely. Add broth and simmer, partially covered, stirring occasionally, until onions and ramps are very soft, about 20 minutes. Stir in ramp greens and boil for 1 minute.

Working in batches, puree soup in a blender until very smooth, about 1 minute per batch, then strain through a fine-mesh sieve into a large heatproof bowl, pressing hard on and then discarding the solids.

Return soup to cleaned pot and bring just to a boil. Whisk in cheese and butter until smooth. Season with salt.

4 servings.

— from Gourmet, *April 2008*

Asparagus, Morels, and Ramp Salad

2 Tablespoons olive oil
¾ pound morel mushrooms, cleaned and cut in half
1 large bunch asparagus spears, blanched
15 ramp stalks, cleaned, trimmed and blanched
Vinaigrette
Chives

In a large nonstick skillet, heat oil until hot. Add morels and cook until golden, 3-4 minutes. Add asparagus and ramps, cooking until slightly warm.

Season to taste with salt and pepper.

Arrange asparagus on plates and add top with morels and ramps. Spoon vinaigrette over it and top with chives.

4-6 servings.

Ramp Hushpuppies

Vegetable oil for deep-frying
2 cups self-rising cornmeal mix
3 Tablespoons self-rising flour
2 Tablespoons finely chopped ramps, both bulbs and stems
1 cup milk
1 egg, beaten

In a deep fryer or heavy, deep skillet, heat 2 to 3 inches of oil over medium heat to 375 degrees. In a mixing bowl, combine cornmeal mix, flour, and ramps. Add milk and egg; mix well. Let stand for 5 minutes.

Drop batter by Tablespoons into hot oil. Fry until golden brown, turning several times. Drain on paper towels.

Makes about 15 hush puppies.

Roasted Chicken, Ramps, and Potatoes

¾ lb ramps
3 lbs chicken, cut into 8 pieces
1 lb small red potatoes, halved
2 ½ Tablespoons olive oil
½ cup dry white whine
1 cup chicken broth

Preheat oven to 450 degrees.

Trim roots from ramps and slip off outer skin on bulbs if loose. Cut off and reserve leaves, leaving white bulbs attached to slender pink stems. Put leaves and bulbs in separate bowls.

Pat chicken dry. Put in a flameproof large shallow roasting pan, without crowding, and surround with potatoes. Drizzle with 2 Tablespoons oil and rub all over to coat evenly. Arrange chicken skin sides up and season with salt and pepper. Roast in upper third of oven for 20 minutes.

Toss bulbs with remaining ½ Tablespoon oil and season with salt. Scatter bulbs around chicken and roast mixture until breast pieces are just cooked through, 10 to 15 minutes.

Transfer breast pieces to a platter and keep

warm. Roast remaining chicken and vegetables 5 minutes more, or until cooked through. Transfer to a platter and keep warm, loosely covered with foil. (If crisper skin is desired, broil chicken only, skin sides up, about 2 minutes.)

Pour off fat from roasting pan and straddle pan across 2 burners. Add wine and deglaze pan by cooking over high heat, scraping up brown bits.

Boil wine until reduced to about ¼ cup and add broth. When broth boils, add ramp leaves and stir until wilted and tender, 1-2 minutes. Remove with tongs and add to chicken. Boil pan juices until reduced to about ½ cup and pour around chicken.

4-6 servings.

White Cheese Pizza with Ramps

For the Dough

1 cup all-purpose flour
1 ½ teaspoons active dry yeast
½ teaspoon salt
¼ teaspoon sugar
¼ cup plus 2 Tablespoons warm water

For the Topping

10 ramps; bulbs, stems, and greens
Extra-virgin olive oil, for brushing
1 cup coarsely grated fresh mozzarella cheese (4 ounces); *see Note*
Salt and freshly ground black pepper
¼ cup freshly grated Parmigiano-Reggiano cheese

The dough:
In a large bowl, whisk the flour together with the yeast, salt and sugar. Pour in the water and stir well with a wooden spoon to form a dough. Scrape the dough out onto a lightly floured work surface and knead for a few minutes until smooth.

Transfer the pizza dough to a lightly oiled large bowl. Cover with plastic wrap or a damp towel and let stand in a warm place until the pizza dough has doubled in bulk, about 1 ½ hours.

Set a pizza stone on the bottom or on the bottom shelf of the oven and preheat to 500 degrees for at least 30 minutes.

The topping:

Bring a medium saucepan of salted water to a boil. Blanch the ramps until they are bright green but still al dente, about 1 minute. Drain, pat dry and cut into 1-inch lengths.

Punch down the pizza dough and transfer it to a lightly floured work surface. Roll out the dough to a 12-inch round, about $1/8$ inch thick. Transfer the dough to a lightly floured, inverted baking sheet. Brush the dough with olive oil and sprinkle on the grated mozzarella in an even layer. Scatter the blanched ramps over the mozzarella and season lightly with salt and pepper. Top the pizza with the Parmigiano-Reggiano cheese.

Slide the pizza onto the hot stone. Bake for about 8 minutes, until the cheese has melted and the pizza crust is browned and crisp on the bottom. Transfer the pizza to a work surface, cut into wedges and serve right away.

8 servings.

— from *Food and Wine*

Grilled Tuna with Ramps, Pinto Beans and Tomato Vinaigrette

4 tuna steaks about 1 inch thick
1 can pinto beans, drained and heated
8 fresh ramps: bulbs, stems, and greens
4 Roma tomatoes
1 Tablespoon rice wine vinegar
1 Tablespoon fresh parsley
2 Tablespoons salt
2 tsp fresh ground black pepper
1 cup extra virgin olive oil

Preheat grill to high.

Toss the tomatoes in ½ Tablespoon of the salt and 1 tsp of the pepper and ¼ cup of the olive oil. Grill over high heat turning often until charred all the way around. Remove from heat and cover in a bowl until soft all the way through.

Combine tomatoes, 1 Tablespoon of salt, 1 tsp of pepper and the rice wine vinegar in a food processor and puree. Slowly add all but one tbsp of the olive oil until well incorporated. Adjust the seasonings and reserve.

Rub the tuna steaks and the ramps with the remaining olive oil, salt and pepper and grill the tuna for only about two minutes per side. The ramps should be grilled for about the same time or until soft.

Place a mound of the (warm) beans in the center of four plates. Slice the tuna into about 5 slices and fan over the beans. Drizzle the vinaigrette around the plate and top everything with two grilled ramps on each plate.

4 servings.

Ramp Pesto

3 to 4 bunches of ramps: bulbs, stems, and greens
1 Tablespoon plus ¾ to 1 cup of olive oil
Salt, to taste
2 Tablespoons walnuts
½ cup parmesan cheese

Separate the ramp stems and bulbs from the leaves. Chop the stems and bulbs into small pieces. Set aside and reserve the leaves.

Heat 1 Tablespoon oil in a small skillet over medium heat. Add the chopped ramp stems and bulbs and cook, stirring occasionally, for about 5 minutes (do not brown).

Mix the ramp leaves, cooked bulbs and stems, salt, walnuts, and ½ cup of oil to the bowl of a food processor. Process until a paste is formed, then drizzle in the rest of the olive oil while continuing to process the mixture. Continue to add more oil until pesto reaches a desired consistency. Taste for salt.

Fold in the Parmesan cheese and serve over pasta.

4 servings.

Spaghetti Sauce with Ramps

½ pound lean ground beef
2 or 3 Italian sausages, chopped
1 large onion, chopped
8-10 ramp bulbs, chopped
1 clove garlic, minced
5 cups marinara sauce or basic spaghetti sauce
1 large can diced tomatoes
1 cup water
1 small can tomato paste
¼ cup minced parsley
1 small bay leaf
Spaghetti
Parmesan cheese

In a large pot, cook ground beef, Italian sausage, and onion until meat is browned. Slice sausages and return to pot. Add ramps and cook for 1 minute longer. Spoon off fat; add the sauce, tomatoes, water, tomato paste, parsley, and bay leaf. Simmer, uncovered, for 30 to 45 minutes. Remove bay leaf. Serve with hot cooked spaghetti and Parmesan cheese.
6 servings.

Ramp Casserole

5 potatoes, diced
3 eggs, beaten
10 ramps, bulbs and stems
1 cup American cheese, diced
½ pound, ground pork sausage
1 cup milk

    Cook potatoes until barely tender. Chop ramps, and add to potatoes for the last few minutes of cooking time.

    Fry the pork sausage, then drain. Combine with eggs, cheese, milk and potatoes and mix thoroughly. Bake in uncovered casserole for 30 minutes at 350 degrees.

    6 servings.

Ramp and Buttermilk Biscuits

3/4 cup chilled buttermilk
3/4 cup thinly sliced trimmed ramps: bulbs, stems, and leaves
1 ½ cups all purpose flour
2 teaspoons baking powder
3/4 teaspoon salt
¼ teaspoon ground black pepper
3/4 stick chilled unsalted butter, cut into pieces
1 large egg, beaten to blend (for glaze)

Preheat oven to 425 degrees.

Mix buttermilk and ramps in small bowl. Mix flour, baking powder, salt, and pepper in processor. Add chilled butter to processor; using pulsating mode, adding butter in pieces, until fine meal forms. Transfer flour mixture to medium bowl. Add buttermilk mixture; stir until dough forms.

Turn dough out onto lightly floured work surface and press out to 6-inch round, about ½ inch thick. Using 2-inch-diameter biscuit cutter dipped in flour, cut out rounds. Gather dough scraps; press out to ½ inch thickness and cut out additional rounds. Transfer dough rounds to baking sheet. Brush biscuit tops with some of egg glaze.

Bake biscuits until golden brown, about 20 minutes. Cool on rack. Serve slightly warm or at room temperature.

Scalloped Potatoes with Ramps

4 medium potatoes, peeled and thinly sliced
Salt and pepper to taste
1 cup coarsely chopped ramps; bulbs, stems, and greens
1 cup milk
1 (4-ounce) package grated Cheddar cheese
Paprika

    Preheat oven to 425 degrees.

    Place a layer of sliced potatoes in a greased 1 ½-quart baking dish. Sprinkle with salt and pepper. Place a layer of ramps on top of potatoes. Continue alternating layers, ending with potatoes as top layer. Pour milk over top. Sprinkle with cheese and paprika.

    Bake for 20-minutes covered at 425 degrees. Uncover and bake an additional 15 minutes or until potatoes are tender.

    6 servings.

Macaroni Salad with Ramps

¾ cup regular, light or low fat mayonnaise
2 Tablespoons cider vinegar
1 Tablespoon prepared mustard
1 teaspoon sugar
1 teaspoon salt
¼ teaspoon pepper
8 ounces elbow macaroni cooked, rinsed with cold water and drained
1 cup sliced celery
1 cup chopped green or red pepper
5 ramps; bulbs, stems, and a few chopped greens

In large bowl combine first 6 ingredients. Add remaining ingredients and toss to coat. Cover and chill for several hours to blend flavors.

Makes 5 cups.

Three-Way Appetizer Spread

2 cups soft white bread crumbs
2 ounce tin water-packed anchovies, drained
1 Tablespoon each lemon zest and lemon juice
½ cup chopped ramps; bulbs and stems
½ teaspoon crushed dry red pepper
¼ cup extra virgin olive oil
Non-fat cottage cheese (for spread or dip only)
1 ½ cups seeded, chopped tomatoes
½ cup chopped cilantro or parsley

    Place first 5 ingredients in food processor fitted with metal blade and pulse until coarsely mixed. With machine on, pour in olive oil plus ¼ cup water. (Add ½ cup non-fat cottage cheese for spread and 1 cup for dip). Chill.

    Just before serving stir in tomato and cilantro. Stuff spread into cherry tomatoes, celery, endive; spread on sliced cucumbers and other vegetables; or serve as a dip with favorite chips.

    Makes 2-3 cups depending on spread or dip.

Crockpot Smothered Steak with Ramps

1 ½ pounds chuck or round steak cut into strips
½ cup flour
1 teaspoon salt
¼ teaspoon pepper
6-8 ramp bulbs, chopped
1 green pepper, sliced
1 pound can tomatoes
1 4-ounce can mushrooms, drained
3 Tablespoons soy sauce

 Put steak strips, flour, salt and pepper in crock pot. Stir well to coat steak. Add remaining ingredients. Cover and cook on high for 1 hour then turn heat to low and cook for 8 hours. Serve over rice.
 6 servings.

Quick Ramp Vichyssoise

½ cup (full measure) dehydrated potatoes
1 can (14-oz) chicken broth
1 pint milk
½ cup finely chopped ramps; bulbs, stems, and a few greens

Mix all ingredients and cook over low heat for 15 minutes, stirring occasionally and adding more milk if needed. Chill and serve.

4-6 servings.

Wilted Lettuce and Ramp Salad

5 cups Bibb lettuce, torn into bite-size pieces
4-6 ramp bulbs, chopped
5 slices bacon, fried crisp and crumbled
2 Tablespoons brown sugar
3 Tablespoons white vinegar
1 Tablespoon water
½ teaspoon salt
¼ teaspoon dry mustard

Put lettuce and ramps in salad bowl. Fry bacon crisp and drain on a paper towel. Cool bacon grease slightly. Add sugar, vinegar, water, salt and mustard. Stir until thickens.

Pour over lettuce and ramps. Sprinkle with crumbled bacon and serve immediately.

6 servings.

Sour Cream Potato Salad with Ramps

7 cups diced, cooked potatoes
½ cup chopped ramps; bulbs and stems
1 teaspoon celery seed
1 ½ teaspoon salt
½ teaspoon pepper
3 hard-boiled eggs

Combine potatoes, ramps, celery seed, salt and pepper, and toss lightly. Separate whites and yolks of egg, reserving yolks for dressing. Chop whites and add to the potato mixture.

Dressing

Egg yolks
1 cup sour cream
½ cup mayonnaise (may use low fat)
¼ cup white vinegar
1 teaspoon prepared mustard

Mash egg yolks and add other 4 ingredients and mix well. Pour dressing over potatoes and toss lightly. Chill thoroughly before serving.
6-8 servings.

Cream of Potato/Ramp Soup

5 medium potatoes, peeled and diced
5-6 ramps; bulbs and stems chopped fine
dash of pepper
4 Tablespoon Butter
2-3 cups milk (depending on how thick you like your soup)

    Put potatoes and ramps in stockpot and barely cover with water. Stir in salt and pepper and cook covered until tender. Mash in liquid. Add butter and milk, stirring until mixture is well blended and hot. Serve immediately.
    4-6 servings.

Pork Ribs with Ramps and Peppers

3 pounds pork ribs
1 ½ teaspoons salt
¼ teaspoon pepper
8-10 chopped ramp bulbs
2 green peppers, cut in strips
Cooked rice

Preheat oven to 450 degrees.

Cover ribs with cold water; bring to a boil and simmer 10 minutes. Drain; rinse ribs in cold water and place in a roasting pan. Sprinkle with salt and pepper.

Bake in 450 degree oven for 15 minutes; or until lightly browned. Pour off fat and remove meat from bones. Add ramps and peppers to ribs and bake 10 minutes or until ramps and peppers soften. Serve over rice.

6 servings.

Swiss Ramp Quiche

1 cup finely crushed cracker crumbs
4 Tablespoons melted butter
6 slices bacon, cooked crisp and crumbled
4-6 chopped ramps; bulbs only
8 ounces grated Swiss cheese
2 eggs, beaten
¾ cup sour cream
½ teaspoon salt
dash of pepper
½ cup shredded American cheese

    Preheat oven to 375 degrees.
    Combine cracker crumbs and melted butter. Press into 8-inch pie pan to form a crust. Cook bacon, drain and crumble. Reserve 2 Tablespoons of drippings and sauté ramps in it until tender.
    Combine remaining ingredients except American cheese. Pour into pie shell. Sprinkle with American cheese and bake at 375 degrees for 25-30 minutes, or until set. Let stand 5-10 minutes before serving.
    6 servings.

Easy Ramp Flatbreads

1 (16. oz.) refrigerated homestyle buttermilk jumbo biscuits
2 Tablespoons olive oil
8 Tablespoons freshly grated Parmesan cheese
18 teaspoons chopped ramps; bulbs, stems, and green tops
kosher salt
pepper

Preheat oven to 400 degrees.

Separate biscuits into individual rounds. Pour olive oil onto a baking sheet. Dip both sides of the biscuit in oil and arrange on a baking sheet. Using fingertips, press each biscuit into a 4-inch flat circle. Sprinkle each biscuit with 1 Tablespoon Parmesan cheese, 1 ½ teaspoons of chopped ramps, pinch of Kosher salt, and pepper.

Bake at 400 degrees for 10-12 minutes.

8 servings.

Tomato, Spinach and Ramp Penne

8 oz. uncooked multigrain penne pasta
8-10 chopped ramps; bulbs only
½ package (18 oz.) mild Italian sausage, sliced
1 Tablespoon olive oil
2 (14.5 oz.) cans diced tomatoes
1 (6 oz.) package fresh baby spinach leaves
2 Tablespoons chopped fresh basil
¼ cup shredded Parmesan cheese

Prepare pasta according to package directions. Sauté ramps and sliced sausage in hot oil in large nonstick skillet over medium heat until tender. Add tomatoes; bring to a boil and cover. Reduce heat to low and simmer, stirring occasionally about 20 minutes.

Add spinach and basil and cook about 5 minutes more.

Toss with pasta and Parmesan.

6 servings.

Ramp Aioli

One bunch ramps, cleaned, diced and sauteed in olive oil with a little salt
one egg yolk at room temp
juice from half lemon
lightly flavored oil (peanut, corn, vegetable)
salt/pepper

Whisk together yolk, salt, and pepper. Slowly drizzle in oil, drop by drop and increasing volume while whisking constantly. After one cup of oil, whisk in lemon juice and a little more oil if necessary to tighten the sauce. Fold in ramps, chill and serve.

— Courtesy of Mark Toor

Made in the USA
Middletown, DE
01 November 2024